CHRISTIAN PERFECTION
BEFORE WESLEY

A Brief Historical Sketch of the Doctrine from the Early Church to the Days of Wesley

by
WALTER G. HENSCHEN, B.D., M.A.

From the Memorial Edition originally arranged for publication by
William S. Deal, A.B., Th.M.

SCHMUL PUBLISHING COMPANY
NICHOLASVILLE, KENTUCKY

COPYRIGHT © 2016 BY SCHMUL PUBLISHING CO.
All rights reserved. No part of this publication may be reproduced or used in any form or by any means—graphic, electronic, or mechanical, including photocopying, recording, taping, or information storage or retrieval systems—without prior written permission of the publishers.

Churches and other noncommercial interests may reproduce portions of this book without prior written permission of the publisher, provided such quotations are not offered for sale—or other compensation in any form—whether alone or as part of another publication, and provided that the text does not exceed 500 words or five percent of the entire book, whichever is less, and does not include material quoted from another publisher. When reproducing text from this book, the following credit line must be included: "From *Christian Perfection Before Wesley* by Walter G. Henschen, © 2016 by Schmul Publishing Co., Nicholasville, Kentucky. Used by permission."

Published by Schmul Publishing Co.
PO Box 776
Nicholasville, KY USA

Printed in the United States of America

ISBN 10: 0-88019-592-4
ISBN 13: 978-0-88019-592-8

Visit us on the Internet at www.wesleyanbooks.com, or order direct from the publisher by calling 800-772-6657, or by writing to the above address.

Contents

Preface 5
Foreword 7
Introduction 9
Author's Preface 11

I   What Wesley Taught on Christian Perfection ... 13

Part One...19
FROM TIME OF CHRIST TO THE REFORMATION

II   The Time of Christ and the Apostles 21
III   The Church Fathers 23
IV   The Pelagian-Augustinian
      Controversy on Perfection 31
V   The Mystics 37

Part Two...41
From The Reformation to the Time of Wesley

VI   Some Experiences of
      Pre-Reformation Leaders 43

VII	The Period of the Reformation Proper 51
VIII	Early Scottish Reformers 55
IX	The Arminians... 57
X	Later Mystics— Madam Guyon, Fenelon 61
XI	Other Eminent Christian Worthies who Helped to Prepare the Way for Wesleyan Christian Perfection 67
XII	The Moravian Pentecost 77

Conclusion 87
Bibliography 89

Preface

How happy we are to see this small but powerful book on *Christian Perfection Before Wesley* presented to the holiness movement again. It has been an interesting study of mine to trace the concepts and ideals of Christian Perfection from the Early Church to the time of John Wesley. Believing that he did not invent the doctrine, but rather that it was clearly presented from the Holy Scriptures, I felt that its thread could be traced throughout early church history previous to Wesley, even through the Dark Ages. The book you hold in your hand, by Rev. Walter Henschen, is a perfect scan and summary of this thread, giving many quotes from primary sources of the Early Church Fathers and later leaders.

As I read material on the subject, I found references to Rev. Walter Henschen's *Christian Perfection Before Wesley* in footnotes and bibliographies, as well as comments about it by authors. Even though it was out of print, it surfaced as a reference often used. Being a colleague and personal friend of Rev. Martha Doubledee, I was aware that she was the author's daughter. Upon inquiry, I found she had a copy, which she loaned for me to read. I was so rewarded as I read it. It is that copy that makes it possible for this reprint.

Rev. Henschen was properly prepared academically for such a book, receiving his B.A. from Olivet Nazarene University, M.A. from Winona Lake School of Theology, and the Bachelor of Divinity from Northern Baptist Theological Seminary. Not only was the author thus recognized in the broader movement, but also served a successful pastoral ministry in the Pilgrim Holiness Church, and had a brilliant tenure as Instructor at God's Bible School, 1947–1952. The last three years of his life, he served as Dean of Theology there. His stalwart place among us as a godly professor of theology certainly had a profound influence upon that generation.

It is hoped that this book will extend his influence currently, as we discover the sound foundations provided herein for the beloved doctrine of Christian Perfection.

May God bless your reading of this gem of a book.

—Rev. John R. Brewer
Fountain City, IN
2016

Foreword

FOR OVER TWENTY-FIVE YEARS it was the writer's pleasure to have known the author of this little volume. Through his efforts he was first introduced to Bible College and to him he owes a considerable debt of gratitude.

Mr. Henschen prepared this work originally in connection with some of his theological studies. He intended to have developed it considerably and to have had it published. But he was a very busy man. Time sped by and before he had done this, he was called to his heavenly reward. Hence, it is presented here much as he left it.

It will be noted that this is a brief *historical* tracing of the doctrine. As such, it does not always present passages from various authors that have perfect *doctrinal* harmony. In the development of doctrines there have been many and long conflicts. There was no exception in the development of the doctrine of Christian Perfection. Readers will allow for this, since this is not a critical analysis, but a short survey of the progress of the doctrine.

The publication of this work has been undertaken on behalf of Mr. Henschen's relatives who wish by this ministry to help him forward the cause which he so dearly loved. This is a highly commendable undertaking on their part.

For over thirty years Mr. Henschen was a teacher, minister and sometimes held administrative positions. He was Dean of Theology of God's Bible School, Cincinnati, Ohio, when he passed away. His life touched and blessed hundreds of young people in his tireless work for the Master.

This little volume is sent forth with the prayer that it may bless a large circle of readers who are interested in the progress of the history of this blessed doctrine.

—Wm. S. Deal

Introduction

THE SUBJECT OF CHRISTIAN PERFECTION has always been, and doubtless will continue to be, one which awakens controversy. This is not an argument against it, but more likely one in its favor, since it treats the subject of God-likeness in a world very un-Godlike.

Christian Perfection or Holiness, whatever it means, is not a new subject, but as old as the Bible. "Be ye holy, for I am holy," is the most exacting imperative ever pronounced upon any creature. If it were an arbitrary command from Creator to creature, carrying with it no Creator obligation or responsibility to help his creature to become and be such, it would be most unjust, cruel and tyrannical. But, if by such help as the Creator may place at the finger tips of his creatures, he may be made what He commands him to be, the imperative is most gracious, and should be welcomed.

Since the subject of Christian Perfection has its beginnings in the Bible, and is so closely related to man's happiness and highest good, it is no wonder that the greatest of religious teachers, all down the centuries should be devoutly interested in it, and should seek to represent it to others, in their best possible way. It is that great period, intervening Wesley and the first century, which is bridged in this treatment.

Any writer who succeeds in throwing light on the subject of Christian Perfection does his readers a good service. This, the author of this volume has sought to do, and the readers will be the judge as to his accomplishment.

Anything that Walter Henschen attempted was done conscientiously and to the best of his ability. He was a plodding, thorough-going student, and one who was well acquainted with sacrifice. He was heroic, for during much of the time of his ministry he had the handicap of a body not physically strong.

Brother Henschen was an aggressive man, who could see possibilities for progress. Faithful to, and always interested in his church, his record of service is one of initiative and accomplishments. Facing an incurable, lingering disease, he bravely served to the end.

His scholarship, experience and interests qualified this author to write upon the subject, and may God continue his ministry through this volume is my prayer.

—J.A. HUFFMAN, D.D.
President, Winona Lake School of Theology
Winona Lake, Indiana

AUTHOR'S PREFACE

FOR ABOUT A HUNDRED YEARS there has been considerable interest in the doctrine of Christian Perfection; more often called Sanctification or Holiness. The first distinctive emphasis of this doctrine was given by John Wesley and the Methodists.

For probably fifty or seventy-five years this was an outstanding feature of the Methodist church. Later many of their leaders altered their views on the subject until the time came when in many if not most quarters the doctrine was largely neglected. Then certain Methodist and Quaker ministers created renewed interest in the doctrine in connection with other religious reforms, promoting Holiness conventions, camp meetings, periodicals, schools and other organizations throughout the country.

As the Holiness movement progressed it permeated other denominations, drawing many of their leaders from various churches until now there are probably close to a million adherents. They have a score or more of schools, including colleges, Bible schools and seminaries; a number of publishing houses which publish periodicals, books and tracts; charitable institutions and hundreds of foreign missionaries with their institutions. Out of this movement has come distinctive Holiness churches such as the Church of the Nazarene, Pilgrim Holiness Church, the Free Methodist, Wesleyan Methodist, Mennonite Brethren in Christ, Church of God, and the Salvation Army. Other smaller denominations have been organized during this period and have included the doctrine of sanctification as one of their cardinal tenets. There are also various inter-denominational organizations whose chief purpose is to propagate the doctrine.

The historical basis of the doctrine of holiness is the quest of our investigation. We have limited ourselves to the pre-Wesleyan sources, and particularly to those influences which probably influenced Wesley most. There is much doctrinal but little historical matter on the subject. We have gleaned most of our materials from this doctrinal literature, arranging in chronical order the development of the doctrine from the time of the Early Church to the time of Wesley, with particular interest in the periods immediately preceding Wesley. We have not been concerned with Theological criticism. We desire merely to marshal historical data in an orderly manner and let it throw what light it will on the doctrinal phase of what Wesley and the Methodists called Christian Perfection or Sanctification.

Only a brief survey of the outstanding traces of the movement has been practicable for the compass of this thesis. Multiplied pages could have been written on most of the incidents and topics where merely brief treatment has been accorded. And further investigation of certain movements, such as that of the various religious Mystics, would provide more complete information; but the scope of our theme has compelled us to brevity.

Chapter I
What Wesley Taught on Christian Perfection

THE PURPOSE OF THIS STUDY is to trace, historically, the doctrine of Christian Perfection before the days of Wesley. If we are to have any fair comparison and evaluation of Wesley's teachings with the teachings on this subject before his day, it is necessary that a brief, but reasonably comprehensive, statement should be made concerning Wesley's teachings on the subject of Christian Perfection.

Let us hear from Wesley himself, as given in the first part of his book on *A Plain Account of Christian Perfection:* "On Monday, June 25, 1744, our first conference began; six clergymen and all our preachers being present. The next morning we seriously considered the doctrine of sanctification, or perfection. The questions asked concerning it, and the substance of the answers given, were as follows:—

"Question. What is it to be sanctified?

"Answer. To be renewed in the image of God, 'in righteousness and true holiness.'

"*Q.* What is implied in being a perfect Christian?

"A. The loving God with all our heart, and mind, and soul. Deut. 6:5.

"Q. Does this imply that all inward sin is taken away?

"A. Undoubtedly; or how can we be said to be 'saved from all our uncleannesses?' Ezek. 36:29.

"Our second conference began August 1, 1745. The next morning we spoke of sanctification as follows:

"Q. When does inward sanctification begin?

"A. In the moment a man is justified. (Yet sin remains in him, yea, the seed of sin, till he is sanctified throughout.) From that time a believer gradually dies to sin, and grows in grace.

"Q. Is this ordinarily given till a little before death?

"A. It is not, to those who expect it no sooner.

"Q. But may we expect it sooner?

"A. Why not? For, although we grant, (1) That the generality of believers, whom we have hitherto known, were not so sanctified till near death; (2) That few of those to whom St. Paul wrote his epistles were so at that time, nor, (3) He himself at the time of writing his former epistles, yet all this does not prove that we may not be so today."

John Fletcher, who was the chief theologian of the early Wesleyan period, says in the first part of his book on *Christian Perfection*: "We call Christian perfection the maturity of grace and holiness, which established adult believers attain to under the Christian dispensation, and by this means we distinguish that maturity of grace which belongs to the dispensation of the Jews below us, and from the ripeness of glory which belongs to the departed saints above us. Hence it appears that, by Christian Perfection, we mean nothing but the cluster and maturity of the graces which compose the Christian character of the church militant.

"In other words, Christian perfection is a spiritual constellation made up of these gracious stars: perfect repentance, perfect faith, perfect humility, perfect meekness, perfect self-denial, perfect resignation, perfect hope, perfect charity for our visible enemies, as well as for our earthly relations; and, above all, perfect love for our visible God, through the explicit knowledge of our Mediator, Jesus Christ. And as this star is always accompanied by the others, as Jupiter is by his satellites, we frequently use, as St. John, the phrase, 'perfect love' instead of the word 'perfection;' understanding by it the pure love of God shed abroad in the heart of established believers by the Holy Ghost, which is abundantly given them under the fullness of the Christian dispensation" (pp. 9-10, edition of 1861 published by Poe and Hitchcock, Cincinnati).

Dr. Adam Clark, another leading theologian and commentator in the early Methodist church, is quoted by Dr. George Peck in his book on *Christian Perfection* as follows: "The word 'sanctify' has two meanings: 1. It signifies to consecrate, to separate from earth and common use, and to devote or dedicate to God and His service. 2. It signifies to make holy or pure...

"This perfection is the restoration of man to the state of holiness from which he fell, by creating him anew in Christ Jesus, and restoring to him that image and likeness of God which he has lost... Sin defaced this divine image: Jesus came to restore it...

"The word 'perfection' in reference to any person or thing, signifies that such person or thing is complete or finished; that it has nothing redundant, and is in nothing defective. And hence that observation of a learned civilian is at once both correct and illustrative, namely, 'We count those things perfect which want nothing requisite for the end whereunto they were instituted'" (pp 51-53, Peck's *Christian Perfection*).

Dr. Peck summarizes the doctrine as follows: "1. As to the nature of Christian perfection, it is clear, first, that our authors neither hold that it implies perfection in knowledge, nor a perfect fulfillment of the requirements of the Adamic law, that is legal perfection. But, secondly, that it implies simply loving God with all the heart. 2. That entire sanctification and Christian perfection are identical. 3. ...When we design, by the term sanctification, to express the state of perfection contended for, we should qualify it by the word entire, or the like.

"4. That the term perfection, signifying the completeness of a thing in the attributes of its kind, considering its circumstances and the purposes of its being, admits of various degrees. Consequently perfection varies in its character according to the character of its subject; and may vary in its degrees, in subjects of the same class, according to the circumstances of the subject, and its particular designation.

"5. That by being saved from all sin in the present life, we mean, first, from all outward sin— all violations of the requirements of the law of love which relate to our outward conduct, and, secondly, all inward sin... which relate to the intellect, the sensibilities, and the will" (*Christian Perfection*, pp 65).

We will give one more definition which we think makes the Wesleyan Doctrine more concise and clear, that by Bishop Foster in which he says of the person entirely sanctified, that he is in "a state in which he will be entirely free from sin, properly so called, both inward and outward. The process of this work is in this order: beginning with pardon, by which one aspect of sin, that is actual guilt, is wholly removed, and proceeding in regeneration, by which another kind of sin, that is depravity, is in part removed, terminating with entire sanctification, by which the remainder of the second kind, or depravity, is entirely removed" (*Christian Purity*, p. 122, quoted by J. A. Wood in *Perfect Love*, p 36).

From the foregoing statements we are impressed with the high standard of Christian attainment taught by Wesley and his co-laborers and successors. It is not our purpose to enter into a critical discussion of the doctrine of Christian perfection, but rather to note some of the most important experiences and pronouncements of outstanding Christian characters preceding Wesley's day, which were at least similar to, if not identical with that of the Methodists.

Part One
FROM TIME OF CHRIST TO THE REFORMATION

Chapter II
THE TIME OF CHRIST AND THE APOSTLES

1. ZACHARIAS, UNDER THE INSPIRATION of the Holy Ghost, indicated that the coming Redeemer would enable them to serve God "In holiness and righteousness before him all the days of our life," Luke 1:75.

2. John the Baptist spoke of the "baptism with the Holy Ghost and with fire" which Jesus should give as an experience beyond that which followed the "baptism with water unto repentance," or regeneration, Matt. 3:11.

3. The baptism with the Holy Ghost on the Day of Pentecost (Acts 2), with the marked enduement of power, was a notable crisis in the lives and ministry of the Apostles. Likewise the incidents of the believers who accepted Christ under the preaching of Phillip at Samaria, having Peter and John sent to them to instruct and pray for them "that they might receive the Holy Ghost," Acts 8:15; Cornelius and his household (Acts 10) and the believers at Ephesus (Acts 19) are historical events which evidently had to do with a definite enlargement and enrichment of Christian experience.

4. Peter, referring to the experience of Cornelius and his household, said, "God... giving them the Holy Ghost, even as

he did unto us, and put no difference between us and them, purifying their hearts by faith," Acts 15:8-9; thus gives us further light on the nature and effect of those experiences. It is quite natural, therefore, that he should exhort in his second epistle, "But as he which hath called you is holy, so be ye holy in all manner of conversation; Because it is written, Be ye holy for I am Holy," II Pet. 1:15-16.

5. Paul, who wrote the Thessalonians, "And the very God of peace sanctify you wholly; and I pray God your whole spirit and soul and body be preserved blameless unto the coming of our Lord Jesus Christ. Faithful is he that calleth you who also will do it," 1 Thess. 5:23-24; must himself have had the same experience, as he calls them to witness "How holily and justly and unblameably we have behaved ourselves among you that believe," 1 Thess. 2:10.

Chapter III
THE CHURCH FATHERS

WE WILL NOW SURVEY THE TIME following the Apostles and extending to the period of the Pelagian-Augustinian controversy.

1. The Custom of Laying on of Hands for Believers to be Filled with the Holy Spirit.

A very illuminating account of this practice is given by Evangelist J. Gilchrist Lawson in his book, *Deeper Experiences of Famous Christians*, from which we will quote as follows:

"Most of the great Bible scholars and commentators, and most of the great Church historians are agreed upon the fact it was the custom of the early church to pray for all believers to be filled with the Spirit. The usual custom was to baptize the converts, and then the elders would lay hands on them and pray for them to receive the gift of the Holy Ghost. The laying on of hands (in prayer for the Holy Spirit) is mentioned in Hebrews 6:2 as one of the 'first principles,' or foundation principles, of the gospel; and in the case of Paul, the Samaritan disciples, and the Ephesian disciples, we have examples of this early custom. The Holy Ghost came without the laying on of hands on the day of Pentecost, but some think this was because there were then no Spirit filled persons to lay hands on the disciples and pray for them to be filled with the Spirit.

"The Holy Spirit also fell upon Cornelius and his household and friends without the laying on of hands in prayer, and while Peter was preaching to them (Acts 10:44); but some suppose this was because no Jew would lay hands on Gentiles to pray for them to be filled with the Spirit until after God poured his spirit on Cornelius... however this may be, it seems certain that the usual order in the early Christian church was first conversion, then baptism, then the laying on of hands in prayer for the Holy Spirit.

"The laying on of hands in prayer was a very ancient custom, and the early Christians probably adopted it from the Jews... The custom of laying hands on ministers when ordaining them is practiced in the churches to-day... The Greek church and other Eastern churches, the Roman Catholic church, the Lutheran church, the Church of England, and a few smaller churches, still retain a relic of the old apostolic custom in what they call Confirmation services, although it is to be feared that these services are often little more than a mere form. In the confirmation services of all these churches the bishops, or priests, lay hands on the persons confirmed and pray for them to be filled with the Holy Ghost. The mere form, however, amounts to but little unless the Holy Spirit actually comes to dwell within. If He does this either with or without the laying on of hands, there will be new life and power in the experiences of the Christian" (pp 44-46).

2. Testimony of the Church Fathers

Lawson says further, "The early Christian writers, both the Greek and Roman Fathers, testify to the fact that in the second century and later, it was customary for Christians to be filled with the Spirit, just as they were prayed for in Bible times. In the days of Tertullian, who wrote in the second century, it was customary also to anoint the baptised believers with oil before praying for them to be filled with the Spirit. The oil was used as a symbol of the Holy Spirit, as it is used all through the Scriptures…

"Tertullian… in his book on *Baptism*, chapter 6, says, "The Baptised, when they come up out of the bath, are anointed with holy oil, and then the hand is laid upon them with the invocation of the Holy Spirit.' This is clear testimony from one of the earliest Christian writers to show that in his day it was customary to pray for the newly baptized converts to be filled with the Spirit. In the same book, chapter 3, he also says, 'After baptism the hand is imposed, by blessing, calling and inviting the Holy Spirit; then that Holy Spirit willingly descends from the Father upon the bodies that are cleansed and blessed.' Again, in the same chapter, he says, 'In baptism we do not receive the Holy Ghost, but being cleansed by baptismal water, we are disposed for the Holy Spirit under the hand of the minister.'

"That prayer for the Holy Spirit was no mere form in the second century is evident from the testimony of Irenaeus. Writing about the middle of the second century, or about 150 A.D., he tells us that in his time, 'when God saw it necessary, and the church, prayed and fasted much, they did miraculous things, even of bringing back the spirit to a dead man.' pp 51-52.

"Clement of Alexandria, writing about the close of the second century, or soon after apostolic times, tells how the Apostle John delivered a young man to the care of a bishop, who baptized him, and 'afterwards he sealed him with the Lord's signature, as with a safe and perfect guard' (see account in Eusebius, Book III, Chapter 17). The filling of the Spirit is commonly called 'The Lord's seal,' or 'The Lord's signature,' by the early Christian writers... The ceremony of anointing with oil was called signaculum, or sealing. The term 'sealing' was probably derived from Ephesians 1:13, where Paul speaks about the Ephesians being sealed with the Holy Ghost after they had believed. He probably refers to the time when they were filled with the Holy Spirit in answer to his prayer, as recorded in Acts 19, and to other similar experiences. However this may be, it is certain that the early Christian writers called the filling of the Holy Spirit the 'sealing of the Spirit.'"

"The great writer Origen, about A.D. 210, also refers to the custom of praying for the newly baptized to be filled with the Spirit. In his Seventh Homily on Ezekiel, he says, 'The unction of Christ, of holy doctrine, is the oil by which the holy man is anointed, having been instructed in the Scriptures, and taught how to be baptized; then changing a few things he (the minister) says to him, 'Now you are no longer a catechumen, now you are regenerated in baptism; such a man receives the unction of God.'

"Firmilian, writing also in the third century, quoted by Cyprian in Epistle 75, compares St. Paul's 'confirming' of the Ephesians (Acts 19) to the confirming of the people in his own time. Firmilian and St. Ambrose seem to be among the first to use the word 'confirm,' or 'confirmation,' to describe the laying on of hands in prayer for the Holy Spirit. The term doubtless is derived from II Corinthians 1:2, 22, 'Now he which establisheth (or confirmeth as it is rendered in the ancient Latin versions) us with you in Christ, and hath anointed us, is God; who hath also sealed us, and given the earnest of the spirit in our hearts...' In the time of St. Ambrose the Latin word confirmatio, which means confirmation, or establishing, began to be the common word for describing imposition of hands in prayer for the Holy Spirit. The Holy Spirit does confirm, or establish, people; and the word confirmation is a good word to describe the filling of the Holy Spirit; but the word has been used so much to describe what is often a mere form or ceremony administered sometimes by wicked and corrupt popes, cardinals, and bishops, that it has lost much of the simplicity and power of its meaning." *ibid.* pp.53-56.

"St. Ambrose... about A.D. 370, in his book on the Sacraments, chapter 2, calls the reception of the Holy Spirit through imposition of hands and prayer, 'a spiritual seal remaining after baptism that perfection may be had.

"In the writing usually attributed to Dionysius the Areopagite, and probably written about A.D. 600, in The Ecclesiastical Hierarchy, chapter 2, there is a description of how prayer was offered for the baptized, that they might receive the Holy Spirit... Further on we read, 'But even to him who is consecrated in the most holy mystery of regeneration the perfective unction of chrism gives him the advent of the Holy Spirit. The learned Church of England bishop, Jeremy Taylor, in his 'Discourse on Confirmation,' explains how the imposition of hands in prayer for the Holy Spirit came to be known as 'The sacrament of chrism,' which is the term used in the writings just quoted. He says: 'It was very early in the church that to represent the grace which was ministered in confirmation, the unction from above, they used oil and balsam, and so constantly used this in their confirmation that from the ceremony it had the appelation: sacramentum chrismatis (the sacramentum of anointing).'" *Ibid.*, p. 64.

"Oecumenius, in the tenth century, commenting on Hebrews 6:2, calls the laying on of hands for the Holy Spirit 'perfection' (telioteta). No doubt this was given for the 'perfecting of the saints' (Eph. 4:12)." *Ibid.*, p. 66.

This able dissertation from Dr. Lawson we think makes clear that not only the early church believed that regenerated persons needed a further specific baptism of the Holy Spirit, but that even during the "Dark Ages" the church, in ceremony at least, taught and practiced the same thing. To show more clearly that some kind or state of Christian perfection, as well as a special anointing of the Holy Spirit was taught, we quote further from the Fathers, as given by Dr. George Peck in his book, *Christian Perfection*, pp 67-68:

1. "'...By love were all the elect of God made perfect... All the generations from Adam unto this day are passed away; but those who were made perfect in love are in the region of the just, and shall appear in glory at the visitation of the kingdom of Christ.' —St. Clement's *Epistle to the Corinthians.*

2. "'Nothing is better than peace, whereby all war is destroyed, both of things in heaven and things on earth. Nothing of this is hid from you, if ye have perfect faith in Jesus Christ, and love, which are the beginning and the end of life: faith is the beginning, love the end; and both being joined in one, are of God. All other things pertaining to perfect holiness follow. For no man that hath faith sinneth; and none that hath love hateth any man.' —St. Ignatius' Epistle to the Ephesians.

3. "Irenaeus, a celebrated father of the second century, says, 'The apostle, explaining himself in his First Epistle to the Thessalonians, chap. V, exhibited the perfect and spiritual salvation of man, saying, But the God of peace sanctify you perfectly; that your soul, body and spirit may be preserved without fault to the coming of the Lord Jesus Christ. How then, indeed, did he have the cause in these three, (that is, to pray

for the entire and perfect preservation of soul, body and spirit, to the coming of the Lord,) unless he knew the common salvation of *these* was the renovation of the whole three? Wherefore he calls those *perfect* who present the three faultless to the Lord. Therefore those are perfect who have the spirit and perseverance of God, and have preserved their souls and bodies without fault.'

4. "But of all the fathers, Macarius, the Egyptian, writes most specifically and consistently upon the subject. He, in his Homilies, treats the subject of set purpose. He says: 'One that is rich in grace, at all times, by night and by day, continues in a perfect state, free and pure, ever captivated with love, and elevated to God...' In like manner Christians, though outwardly they are tempted; yet inwardly they are filled with the divine nature, and so nothing injured. These degrees, if any man attain to, he is come to the perfect love of Christ, and to the fulness of the Godhead.

"'As iron, or lead, or gold, or silver, when cast into the fire, is freed from that hard consistency which is natural to it... after the same manner the soul that has renounced the world, and fixed its desires only upon the Lord, and hath received that heavenly fire of the God-head, and of the love of the Spirit, is disentangled from all love of the world, and from all the corruption of the affections... For when the soul is thoroughly cleansed from all its corrupt affections, and is united with an ineffable communion to the Spirit, the Comforter, and is thoroughly mixed with the Spirit, and is become spirit itself; then it is all light, all eye, all spirit, all joy, all rest, all gladness, all love, all bowels, all goodness, and clemency... being blameless within and without, and spotless, and pure; for being brought to perfection by the Spirit, how is it possible that they should outwardly produce the fruits of sin? Sin is rooted out by the coming of the Holy Spirit, and man receives the original formation of Adam in his purity...

"'What, then, is that "perfect will of God" to which the apostle calls and exhorts every one of us to attain? It is perfect purity from sin, freedom from shameful passions and the assumption of perfect virtue; that is the purification of the heart by the plenary and experimental communion of the perfect and divine spirit. To those who say that it is impossible to attain unto perfection, and the final and complete subjugation of the passions, or to acquire a full participation of the Good Spirit, we must oppose the testimony of the divine scriptures; and prove to them that they are ignorant, and speak both falsely and presumptuously.'" Wesley was especially influenced by Macarius and included a portion of his *Homilies* in his Christian Library, vol. 18.

Rev. H.A. Baldwin makes the statement in an article published in *The Free Methodist*, January 22, 1932, on "Entire Sanctification A Biblical, Historical and Experimental Fact," No. 2, that "Wesley says that it was the reading of the remarkable description of a perfect Christian given by Clement of Alexandria which inspired him to write his tract, 'The Character of A Methodist' (Journal, March 4, 1769). Clement's 'Exhortation to the Heathen,' his 'Instructor' and the 'Stromata' are among the most valuable productions which have come down to us from Christian antiquity. A volume might be written setting forth the experimental theology of Clement, beginning with the new birth and comprising every step until the consummation in Christian perfection."

We could give many more quotations from the Fathers along the same line as the above, but we believe we have given enough to show the doctrine of Christian perfection was held by many of the church fathers.

Chapter IV
THE PELAGIAN-AUGUSTINIAN CONTROVERSY ON PERFECTION

THE CONTROVERSY BETWEEN Pelagius and Augustine in the fifth century seems to have been the beginning of the main differences of opinion which have divided the church ever since on the subject of sin and the extent and manner of victory over it. As in most controversies, both sides went to opposite extremes— unfortunately for succeeding generations.

Dr. George Peck says, "Pelagius maintained that the will is naturally free to do good, and is not at all impaired by the fall; that there are no special influences of the Spirit in regeneration, but all the helps that are necessary in that work is instruction, and that man can by this aid perfectly keep the law... Pelagius was brought before a council of fourteen bishops belonging to Palestine, at Diospolis, (Lydda,) A.D. 415, to answer to sundry charges. Charge VI is, 'Pelagius has said that man may be without sin.' To this Pelagius responds, 'I have indeed said that man may be without sin, and keep God's commandments, if he will. For this ability God has given him. But

I have not said that any one can be found, from infancy to old age, who has never sinned, but being converted from sin, by his own labor and God's grace he can be without sin; still, he is not by this immutable for the future" (*Christian Perfection,* pp 90-91).

The same writer quotes from Professor Wiggers as follows: "'Augustine himself, in his earliest writing against the Pelagians, (De Pec. Mer. II, 6; De Spir. et Lit. 1,) had granted, nay, even defended, the position, (taken in the abstract as the Pelagians took it,) that, by God's grace, man may be without sin. And though he did not himself believe, that anyone *is* without sin in this life, (De Pec. Mer. II, 7,) still he did not regard this as a dangerous opinion, provided only that one does not believe we can attain it by our own power. (De Spir. et Lit. 2; De Nat. et Gr. 60.) I know this is the opinion of some, (viz., that there have been, or are, men without sin,) whose opinion in this matter I dare not censure, though I cannot defend it, De. Perf. Just, Hom. 21.' In the letter of the five bishops to Innocent, as well as in several of the early pieces of Augustine, this position was left doubtful, or at least pronounced a sufferable error... Even Ambrose had held to it, in a certain sense. And in his book On the Acts of Pelagius, c. 30, written soon after, Augustine numbers this question, both in the abstract and in the concrete, among those which are not to be denied as though already decided in opposition to the heretics, but to be kindly discussed among the Catholics. But, after this synod, (in C. d Epp. Pel. IV, c 10,) he represents this opinion as a dangerous and detestable error. He does not, however, here present it in the abstract sense in which the Pelagians really held it, but as if they maintained that there were and had been righteous men who, in this life, had no sin. And from this time onward, as appears from C. Jul. IV, 3, he could not endure the doctrine of man's ability to be without sin" *(Historical Presentation,* p. 174).

Peck adds, "It should be carefully considered that the perfection for which Pelagius contended was a *legal perfection—* perfect conformity to the demands of the law of innocence. It also appears that he entertained the notion that 'the grace of God is given according to our merits'— that 'the merit of good-will precedes grace.' He says: 'When man is divinely aided, he is aided for the purpose of attaining perfection.— The nature of man is good which deserves the aid of such grace.' *Ibid.,* pp. 189, 190.

"Here is a specific statement from authentic sources of the Pelagian system. But a slight examination of it will convince any unprejudiced mind that the system is but little understood, and that too frequently Pelagianism is charged upon those who are even farther from that heresy than those who bring the charge... It will have been observed, that he (Augustine) sometimes denies, and at other times admits, that men can live without sin. And hence both those who assert and those who deny the doctrine of perfection often quote him as authority. The learned professor who has furnished the principal part of my materials upon the Pelagian controversy, advertises of a change in the opinions of Augustine, as to the possibility of keeping the law, after the Council of Carthage. But the fact is, that, so early as this period, the distinction between mortal and venial sins, which occupies so prominent a place in Romish theology, had obtained. And Augustine... held this... to be a catholic verity" *(Christian Perfection,* pp. 96-98).

Farther on in his discussion of the question in hand, Peck summarizes a treatment of the subject by Bishop Jewell, in which he, Peck, says, "That these fathers evidently, after all their zeal against the Pelagian error of perfection, acknowledge,— as all, indeed, who reverence the Scriptures are forced to do— a qualified perfection to be predicable of men on earth" (p. 108).

To the same point, Rev. H.A. Baldwin contributed a series of illuminating articles in the *Free Methodist* on the subject, "Entire Sanctification, A Biblical, Historical and Experimental Fact." In Part 3, January 29, 1932, he has this to say regarding Augustine and Christian Perfection: "In his early writings Augustine acknowledged that one might be made holy. His change of mind came about in this way: Augustine always taught that membership in the orthodox church was a necessity to salvation. When the Donatists dissented from the orthodox church, because of its declining spirituality, Augustine attacked them with great bitterness. He could not oppose a movement for a supposed wrong and acknowledge a possible right. One of the leading tenets of the Donatists was Christian perfection; this must go along with all other supposed errors. (Wesley says the Donatists were the Methodists of their day.) The departure of Augustine from the doctrine of perfection was completed in his savage onslaught on Pelagius, whom he accused of teaching that man could by his own will make himself holy. Pelagius denied this charge, but the denial made no change in Augustine's opposition. (Wesley says that as far as he could discern, Pelagius was one of the holiest men of his day.)

"That Augustine at one time acknowledged the possibility of holiness is seen in the following, taken from his *Confessions*, which were composed ten years after his conversion and years before the Pelagian controversy. 'Can it at any time or place be an unrighteous thing for a man to love God with all his heart, with all his soul, and with all his mind, and his neighbor as himself?' —*Confessions*, Book III, Chap. 8.

"In his book, *On the Forgiveness of Sins*, Book II, chap. 7, he acknowledges the possibility of living without sin, but denies that any person lives who succeeds in so doing. A friend, named Marcellinus, was much disturbed by such a statement and wrote him to this effect. Augustine replied by writing his book, *On the Spirit and the Letter*, in which he restated his proposition and added that any who thought they could attain to such a height without the grace of God were in error, but adds, 'If, however, anybody... shall have proved that some man or men have spent a sinless life upon earth, whoever does not, not merely refrain from opposing him, but also does not rejoice with him to the full, is afflicted with extraordinary goads of envy' (chapters 1-3).

"In his book, *On Man's Perfection in Righteousness*, chapter 21, Augustine states that there were some whose views he did not have the 'courage to censure' who believed that singleness was a possible experience.

"Augustine occupies the unenviable position of being the first among the church fathers to come out squarely against the doctrine of deliverance from inward sin. John Fletcher calls him the 'father of rigid imperfectionists.'

"In his book *On the Spirit and the Letter*, chapters 65 and 66, he states that there is no man living on the earth 'who is absolutely free from all sin.' His argument in this place amounts to this— God can, but will not... In this connection he also states that no man can hope in this life to attain to the fullness of love enjoyed by those on the other side, but they can reach a place where they will be swayed by no lust. These citations sufficiently illustrate the confusion which existed in the mind of this great man with reference to the doctrine of Christian perfection."

It is quite evident that some form of Christian perfection was taught by the church fathers all the way from the earliest centuries to and through the Middle Ages. The Pelagian-Augustinian controversy was taken up again with fervid zeal by the Arminians and their opponents during the seventeenth century, which we will note later on when dealing with the Arminians.

Chapter V
THE MYSTICS

WHEN WELL MEANING, pious souls wanted to get away from the world during the corruption of the Roman Catholic church, many of them formed various orders and adopted plans and methods by which they tried to cultivate holy living. Among these were different orders of what are known as the "Mystics," some of whom no doubt attained to a high degree of piety and holiness. We do not approve of some of their ascetic practices but we do commend their earnest desire and effort to live a holy life. There can be no doubt about the earnestness and sincerity of many of them of whom God certainly took note and gave them "the desire of their heart." We believe the promise was fulfilled to them which says, "Blessed are they which do hunger and thirst after righteousness: for they shall be filled" (Matt. 5:6).

The place of the Mystics in contributing to the development of the doctrine of Christian perfection is aptly stated by Rev. J.P. Taylor in an article in the *Free Methodist*, December 4, 1932, on the subject, "Holiness— The Doctrine of Antiquity," in Part 1 of which he says: "For some years before Wesley's time the holy waters had been gliding silently through the homes and assemblies of the Mystics in England, the Pietists in Germany, and the Quietists in Spain, Italy and France. It was from such sources that Wesley first 'caught the singing of the waters.' There were some foreign elements of a dangerous tendency in the teachings of these groups, but a perfect process of filtration took place, as the truth poured through the capacious soul and discerning mind of the great founder of Methodism."

In his book on *Scriptural Sanctification*, Dr. John R. Brooks quotes from Dr. Gordon, who, after commenting on the wonderful baptism of the Holy Ghost received by the devout and distinguished church historian, Merle D'Aubigné, says: "Here indeed was a most blessed experience; but not something strange and exceptional in religious biography. We can trace the same thing under different names through many saintly lives. The 'inward death' of Mysticism; the 'divine stillness' of Quietism; the 'rest of faith' of the Brethren of the Higher Life— all these terms are readily translated back into the one idea of the peace of God ruling in the heart. It is, in a word, the perfect quiet which comes to the soul that is yielded up in perfect self-surrender to God. Tauler is constantly describing it as the fountain of that wonderful second life of his after his two years' retirement from the pulpit into the cell. 'If man truly loves God,' says he, 'and he has no will but to do God's will, the whole force of the River Rhine may run at him and will not disturb him or break his peace'" (pp. 219-220).

Brooks adds, with reference to Tauler, "In speaking of this experience, Tauler says that its possessor enjoys 'the most quiet and peaceful liberty, being uplifted above all fear and agitation of mind concerning death and hell, or any other things which might happen to the soul either in time or in eternity.'"

Many more interesting experiences of the Mystics could be given for which we do not care to give space now. Later on we will give the experiences of some later Mystics such as Madam Guyon, Fenelon, Fox, etc.

Part Two
From The Reformation to the Time of Wesley

Chapter VI
SOME EXPERIENCES OF
PRE-REFORMATION LEADERS

1. GIROLAMO SAVONAROLA, OF ITALY, was one of the greatest reformers, preacher, prophets, politicians, and philosophers the world has ever known. His public career as a preacher began the same year that Luther was born; and someone has said that if the soil of Italy had been as congenial as that of Germany to a Protestant Reformation, he instead of Luther might have been the instrument in God's hands for that reformation. As it was, Savonarola was the precursor of the Reformation. By his terrific denunciation of the corruptions of the Catholic church, he prepared Europe for Luther's work.

Savonarola was born in Ferrara, Italy, September 14, 1452. His parents were cultured but worldly people. From his infancy he had been quiet and retiring. At an early age he became a very diligent student, and he afterwards attained great proficiency in the liberal arts and in philosophy. He was an earnest student of Aristotle but the writings of the great Greek philosopher left the soul unsatisfied. The philosophy of Plato gave him a little more satisfaction; but it was not until he began to study the writings of Thomas Aquinas that he found real food for his soul. It was doubtless the writings of that great saint which led Savonarola, at a very early age, to yield his whole heart and life to God; and the works of Aquinas probably continued to influence his life more than any other writings outside of the Scriptures.

As a boy his devotion and fervor increased as he grew older, and he spent many hours in prayer and fasting. Disgusted with the corruption of the age he decided to enter the monastic life, entering a Dominican convent April 24, 1475. Here he fasted and prayed, led a silent life, and became increasingly absorbed in spiritual contemplation. His modesty, humility and obedience surpassed that of all others. Soon after entering the convent he was made a lecturer on philosophy to the monastery, which position he held during the remainder of the years that he spent there.

In 1481 Savonarola went to the convent of St. Mark's in Florence, the most beautiful and cultured city in Italy, and the city where he was to become famous. The Renaissance, or revival of learning, had affected Florence more than any other place. The next year after entering the convent he was made instructor of the novices, and finally raised to the rank of preacher in the monastery. Although the monastery had a splendid library Savonarola came more and more to use the Bible as his text book. He was filled with a sense of approaching judgment, terror and the vengeance of God, and often gave vent to his feelings when sent to preach in the neighboring towns. But his preaching had so little effect either in Florence or the surrounding towns, that he decided to give up preaching and confine himself to teaching the novices.

In 1482 Savonarola was sent to Reggio d'Emilia, to represent his convent in a Dominican chapter-general. During the first day, while the monks were discussing dogma, he remained silent. But the second day, when a question of discipline came up, he arose and in powerful accents denounced the sins and corruption of the church and clergy. His soul was stirred and he spoke with an eloquence which made a profound impression. Returning to Florence he could not refrain from preaching. But his sermons made little impression on the pleasure loving Florentines.

It was about this time that this reformer had a wonderful experience that revolutionized his life and ministry. In prayer and meditation he waited upon God, and yearned for a revelation direct from Him. One day, while engaged in a conversation with a nun, he suddenly beheld in a vision the heavens opened, and the future calamities of the church passed before his eyes; and he seemed to hear a voice charging him to announce them to the people. "From that moment," says Lawson, "he was convinced of his divine mission, and was filled with a *new unction and power*. His preaching was now with a voice of thunder, and his denunciation of sin so terrific that the people who had listened to him sometimes went about the streets half-dazed, bewildered and speechless. His congregations were often in tears, so that the whole church resounded with their sobs and weeping. Men and women of every age and condition, workmen, poets, philosophers, would burst into passionate tears. Pico della Mirandola tells of a sermon of Savonarola's which, 'made a cold shiver run down his back, and made his hair stand on end.'

"Savonarola's ardor for prayer, his faith, and his devotion increased day by day. His companion, Fra Sebastiano of Brescia, says that Savonarola, when engaged in prayer, frequently fell into a trance, and was sometimes so transported by holy fervor that he was obliged to retire to some solitary place. Some of his biographers relate that on Christmas Eve, in the year 1486, Savonarola, while seated in the pulpit, remained immovable for five hours, in an ecstacy, or trance, and that his face seemed illuminated to all the church, and that this occurred several times afterward. Savonarola told his friend and biographer, the younger Pico della Mirandola, that on one occasion while meditating on the text, 'Blessed art Thou O Lord; teach me thy statutes,' he felt his mind illuminated, and all doubts left him, and he felt more certainty of the things that were shown him than a philosopher did of first principles.

"In 1484 Savonarola was sent as Lenten preacher to the little republic of San Gimignano. Here he preached with such power that he returned to Florence with greater confidence in his mission... he was sent to preach in various cities of Lombardy, especially in Brescia. Everywhere he went his denunciations of sin awakened much alarm, and his fame continued to spread over Italy... In 1489 he returned to Florence, the Lord revealing to him that great things awaited him there. He began to explain the book of Revelation to the friars, in the garden of St. Mark's convent. But his fame had spread through Florence; and laymen begged for admittance to his lectures. His congregations increased daily until he had to preach from the pulpit of the church. The church was thronged for the first service, and many stood or clung to the iron gratings in order to see and hear the preacher. The voice of Savonarola seemed to have almost a superhuman effect, and the audience was raised to a transport of ecstasy. After that service all Florence spoke of Savonarola, and even the most learned flocked to hear him. By Lent of 1491 San Marco church had become too small to hold the people, and Savonarola moved to the famous Duomo, or cathedral church of Florence, where he remained during the remainder of the eight years which was the limit, as he predicted it would be, of his preaching in Florence. The people were so anxious to hear him that they arose in the middle of the night, and waited for hours for the cathedral doors to open. They came along the street singing and rejoicing and listened to the sermons with such interest that when they were finished the people thought they had scarcely begun. Savonarola seemed to be swept onwards by a might not his own, and carried his audiences with him. Soon all Florence was at the feet of the great preacher...

"The people of Florence abandoned their vile and worldly books, and read Savonarola's sermons. All prayed, went to church, and the rich gave freely to the poor. Merchants restored ill-gotten gains amounting to many florins. Even the hoodlums, or street gamins, stopped singing ribald songs, and sang hymns instead. All the people forsook the carnivals and vanities in which they had indulged, and made huge bonfires of their masks, wigs, worldly books, obscene pictures, and other things of the kind. The children marched from house to house in procession singing hymns, and collecting everything they styled vanities... A bonfire was made of this amidst the singing of hymns and pealing of bells...

"But the triumph of Savonarola was short. During his first sermon in Florence, he predicted that he would only preach there eight years. He also foretold his own martyrdom. Although people from all over Italy flocked to Florence to hear him, until the great Duomo itself would not hold the crowds, his fearless sermons aroused the anger of many, and especially of the corrupt pope, cardinals, and priests. He was threatened, excommunicated, and persecuted; and finally, in 1498, by express order of Alexander VI, he was burned to death in the public square of Florence, the city he loved so well. His last words were, 'The Lord hath suffered so much for me.' Thus perished one of the world's greatest saints and martyrs." —*Deeper Experiences of Famous Christians*, pp. 79-84.

2. John Wyclif, who died about 1384, is quoted by Dr. George Peck in his *Christian Perfection*, pp. 70-71, as follows: "To be turned from the world, is to set at naught, and to put out of mind, all likings, joys, and mirths thereof, and to suffer meekly all bitterness, slanders, and troubles thereof, for the love of Christ, and to leave all occupations unlawful and unprofitable to the soul, so that man's will and thought be dead to seek anything that the world seeketh and loveth. Therefore the prophet speaketh in the person of the soul's perfectly turning to God, saying, Mine eyes, that is, my thought and intent, shall ever be to God. For he shall draw my feet, that is, my soul and affections, out of the snare, and the net of the love of this world. He that is truly turned to God, fleeth from vices, beholdeth not the solaces or comforts of this world; but setteth his mind so steadfastly on God, that he well nigh forgetteth all outward things; he gathereth himself all within; he is reared up wholly unto Christ.' —*Of Perfect Life*— Writings of Rev. and learned John Wickliffe: one of the volumes of the English reformers published by the Religious Tract Society."

3. "'Erasmus, on Matt. v. 8 says,'" quotes Peck again, p. 71, "'how much more blessed be they who, being delivered from blindness of the mynde, have the gift inwardly to see God. As the sunne is to cleare eyes, so is God to pure and cleane mindes... Therefore blessed be they, whose heart is *pure and clean from all filthyness*. For they shall have this gift, which is more to be desired than all the pleasures of the world: they shall see God.' —Paraphrase. This paraphrase was translated by order of Henry VIII into English, and ordered to be placed

in the churches. My copy is in black letter, and may be the original edition; but this I cannot certainly determine, as the title page is wanting."

4. Thomas à Kempis— 1380-1472,— as is well known wrote those immortal works which influenced Wesley in seeking to live a holy life.

Chapter VII
THE PERIOD OF THE REFORMATION PROPER

THE MAIN BURDEN of the Reformers was to revive the doctrine of "justification by faith" and deliver the church from a mere form of worship in its ritualism and ceremony, to a simple direct worship of God "in spirit and in truth." To oppose the Roman Catholic doctrine of perfection through Works of "supererogation," Luther, Calvin and many others resorted to the dogmas of Augustine on the necessity of sin and imperfection in this life. It seems that it was the work of Luther, in the providence of God, to revive the doctrine of justification; and it was the work of Wesley to revive the doctrine of sanctification or Christian perfection. The church in the time of the early reformers was hardly in an adequate condition to receive this deeper teaching of a "higher life." The Reformers did their work well— they fulfilled their mission. They rescued the fundamental and basic doctrine of justification by faith; they restored the Scriptures to and for the masses; they broke down superstition and ritualism; they purified the church of corruption— all of which was a necessary preparation for the development of the higher life of entire sanctification and holiness.

Although Luther and Calvin were influenced by Augustinian imperfection, yet they at times gave vent to expressions along the line of the higher experience. In an editorial in the *Herald of Holiness*, May 25, 1932, the statement is made that Luther, "In his definition of the church he says, 'They are called a Christian people, and have the Holy Ghost, who daily sanctifies them, not only by the forgiveness of sin, but also by the laying aside, expelling and destroying of sin, and hence they are called a holy people.'"

Dr. Peck says: "The only passage in the Augsburg Confession which has any reference to the subject under discussion is the following:— 'They condemn the Pelagians, and others, who teach that it is possible, by the sole power of reason, without the aid of the Holy Spirit, to love God above all things, and do His commandments.'

"It is clear that the Augsburg Confession, and its great defender, direct their opposition, not against the Wesleyan theory of evangelical perfection, but the *graceless* theory of Pelagians, and the legal system of the Romanists. The expressions of Melancthon upon the subject of the remaining corruptions of 'the regenerate' are not a whit stronger than those of Mr. Wesley, which he gives us in his sermon 'On Sin in Believers.' The difference seems to be that Mr. Wesley makes a *general*, and Melancthon a *universal* application of his doctrine to the actual state of Christians.

"But in addition to their Confession of Faith, the reformers also submitted to the Diet a list of corruptions which had crept into the Roman Church and which they had corrected. Chap. VI is 'of monastic vows;' and contains the following distinct and explicit admission of the doctrine of perfection:— 'Those therefore who would be justified by their vows, have abandoned the grace of God through Christ;

for they rob Christ of his glory, who alone can justify us, and transfer this glory to their vows and monastic life. It is moreover a corruption of the divine law and of true worship, to hold up the monastic life to the people as the only perfect one. For Christian perfection consists in this, that we love and fear God with all our heart, and yet combine with it sincere reliance and faith in him through Christ: that it is our privilege and duty to supplicate the throne of grace for such things as we need in all our trials, and in our respective callings, and to give diligence in the performance of good works. It is in this that true perfection consists, and the true worship of God, but not in begging, or in a black or white cap'" (*Christian Perfection*, pp. 116-117).

The *Theologia Germanica* which Luther prized so highly gives the following stages by which the soul attains unto perfection:

I. "The purification concerneth those who are beginning or repenting, and is brought to pass in a threefold wise:

(1) "By contrition and sorrow for sin,

(2) "By full confession,

(3) "By hearty amendment.

II. "The enlightening belongeth to such as are growing, and also taketh place in three ways: to-wit,

(1) "By eschewal of sin,

(2) "By the practice of virtue and good works,

(3) "And the willing endurance of all manner of temptation and trials.

III. "The union belongeth to such as are perfect, and also is brought to pass in three ways: to-wit,

(1) "By pureness and singleness of heart,

(2) "By love,

(3) "And by the contemplation of God, the Creator of all

things."—Chapter 14. [The numbering is our own.]

A prayer adopted by the Reformers goes thus: "Cleanse the thoughts of our hearts by the inspiration of thy Holy Spirit, that we may perfectly love Thee, and worthily magnify thy Holy name, through Jesus Christ our Lord." This prayer was no doubt answered in the hearts of the many earnest souls who prayed it.

Chapter VIII
Early Scottish Reformers

As would naturally be expected the Scottish reformers were influenced by Augustine's theology, but there were also expressions along the line of the higher life which had a trend toward Wesleyan theology. This is shown by James Alex McDonald in his *Wesley's Revision of the Shorter Catechism*. After stating in his Preface that Wesley was influenced by Scottish piety, among other things through Henry Scougal's *Life of God in the Soul of Man*, he says, "This 'Life of God in the Soul of Man' is the essence of true Christianity. It is the secret of Pentecost... This experience of perfect love has not been unknown to many of our most useful Scottish saints, among whom it was sometimes called the 'rest of faith,' 'the full assurance of faith.'"

This author quotes from Patrick Hamilton in these words, "He that loveth God keepeth all His commandments. He that hath faith keepeth all the commandments of God," and then adds, "Wesley's work was twofold. By preaching justification by faith he reaffirmed the Reformation doctrine... Preaching entire sanctification by faith he reaffirmed and developed the early Reformation doctrine of

Holiness as maintained by Patrick Hamilton" (p. 85).

In this connection we wish to refer to another statement made by McDonald in his Preface, regarding Wesley and the *Shorter Catechism*, "As far as we can judge, there is but one sentence in the whole Confession (1560) which Wesley's followers might wish to improve— the work of the Holy Spirit, in the sanctification of believers, should have a fuller expression, such as Knox has himself admitted, by incorporating the 'Places' of Patrick Hamilton in his History of the Reformation. It appears to us that Hamilton has expressed in a most thoroughgoing manner the doctrine of holy living, which was the secret of the great Methodist revival."

Robert Blair, one of the founders of the Presbyterian church in Ireland, quoted in *Scot's Worthies*, is repeated by McDonald as saying, "'I perceive that many who make a right use of faith in order to attain unto the knowledge of justification make no direct use of it in order to sanctification. And that the living of the just by faith reacheth further than I formerly conceived, and that the heart is purified by faith. I had not learned to make use of faith as a means and an instrument to draw holiness out of Christ... I saw it was no wonder this occasioned an obstruction in the progress of holiness, and I perceived that making use of Christ for sanctification without directly employing faith... was like one seeking water out of a deep well without a long cord to let down the bucket and draw it up again...'" (pp. 90-91).

Chapter IX
The Arminians

1. Arminius.

A RMINIUS AND HIS CO-LABORERS in the seventeenth century were charged by Gomarus with holding "the perfection of men in this life." This charge called forth from Arminius a specific statement of his views, in which Dr. Peck says, "It seems, he did not profess to differ from the *earlier and more sober views* of Augustine upon the subject. He says,—

"'Besides those things of which I have already spoken, much has often been said concerning the perfection of believers, or the regenerate, in this life, and it is reported that I hold views on this subject which are improper, and almost the same as those of the Pelagians, viz., that the regenerate can in this life perfectly observe the precepts of God. To this I reply, that I ought not, on this account, to be considered either partially or wholly a Pelagian, even if I held this view; provided that I should make this addition,— that they could do this by the grace of Christ, but by no means without it. Yet I have never said that a believer can in this life perfectly observe the precepts of Christ, nor have I ever denied it, but have left it entirely undetermined...'" (*Christian Perfection*, p. 132).

2. Episcopius.

We again quote in part from Peck, "The following account of the opinions of Episcopius, the eloquent successor of Arminius in the divinity chair of the university of Leyden, is taken from his answer to the nineteenth question proposed to him by his pupils in private disputations at Amsterdam:

"Quest. 19. "Be ye therefore perfect even as your Father which is in heaven is perfect," Matt. 5:48. The question is, "What should be understood here by the word perfect? Is it that we should perfectly keep all the commands of God and Christ without any sin, (except those which preceded conversion?) But if so, whether this is necessary for attaining to the life of the blessed."

"Embracing the opportunity afforded by this question, I wish also to answer another— 'Whether a man, assisted by divine grace, can keep all the commands of God, even to a perfect fulfillment, that is, using the word love in a general manner for keeping the commandments, whether he can love as much as he ought to love according to the requirement of the gospel, or according to the covenant of grace?' I, indeed, have no doubt on this point. My reasons are these: 1st. God demands no other love than that which is rendered by the whole mind, the whole heart, and all the strength. Therefore he demands nothing beyond or above the strength. 2nd. God promises that he will circumcize the heart of his people, that they may love Him with their whole heart and mind. Deut. 30:6 3rd. God Himself testifies that there have been those who have kept all His commands all the days of their life with their whole mind, and heart, and strength, and this in the sight of God: as we may read of Asa, 1 Kings 15:14; of the whole people, 2 Chron. 15:12; of David, 1 Kings 11:34, and 14:8, and 15:11; of Josiah, 2 Kings 22:2, that he "Turned to the Lord with all his heart, and with all his soul, and might, according to all the law of Moses," 2 Kings 23:25. And we read that these things were attributed to them by God under the old covenant. Who, then, can doubt that the same thing can have place in the new covenant?

"'The common distinction between a perfection of parts and one of degrees requires explanation... But if by a perfection of degrees is understood that highest perfection which consists in the highest exertion of human strength assisted by divine grace, and which is joined with the purpose of making continual progress in proportion to his increased strength, then I believe there is no reason why it should be said to be impossible to man on the earth...

"...The highest evangelical perfection (for we are not treating of legal perfection, which includes sinlessness entire in all respects...) embraces two things:— 1st. A perfection proportioned to the powers of each individual; 2nd. A desire of making continual progress, and of increasing one's strength more and more. This perfection varies in respect to beginners, proficients, and those perfect in the knowledge of divine truth, and of that love which is required of us: for which reason there is one perfection higher than another, or the perfection of some is higher than the perfection of others...'" *(Christian Perfection*, pp. 134-136).

3. Limborch.

Dr. Peck quotes from the learned Limborch, who gives us his views on the subject in hand:

"'The possibility of keeping the commandments of our Saviour is taken for granted by what has been said of the necessity thereof; since things necessary must be observed, but impossibilities cannot... a man may, by the assistance of God's grace, keep the precepts commanded in the gospel, after such a manner, and in such a degree of perfection, as God requires of us under the denunciation of eternal damnation... not a sinless or absolutely perfect obedience, but such as consists in a sincere love and habit of piety, which excludes all habit of sin, with all enormous and deliberate actions... Besides, we do not say a man can live blameless without falling into any sin... but this we do assert, that we ought to proceed in a Christian course, to amend our failings, to watch against temptations, till at last we arrive to perfection, and by the grace of God attain everlasting life'" (*Ibid*, pp. 136-143).

Chapter X
Later Mystics— Madam Guyon, Fenelon

PROBABLY THE MOST DEFINITE experiences and testimonies in the higher Christian life before the time of Wesley come from some of the later Mystics, such as Madam Guyon and Fenelon.

1. Madam Guyon.

Madam Guyon was probably converted at four years of age, experienced various periods of relapses until about 1668, when she was definitely converted. She said, "My heart was quite changed, that God was there; for from that moment he had given me an experience of His presence in my soul... was all on a sudden so altered, that I was hardly to be known either to myself or others." She had great joy in prayer and communion, in which she spent much time, as well as doing practical Christian work for her Lord in visiting and ministering unto the poor and needy.

For about two years she enjoyed this wonderful experience, then she was drawn away to some extent into worldly conformity. Her chief temptation was in worldly dress and conversation. This brought her to deeper reflection, and created a hunger for a deeper and more victorious Christian experience. J. Gilchrist Lawson in his book, *Deeper Experiences of Famous Christians*, tells how she attained this longing of her heart:

"One day as she was walking across one of the bridges of the river Seine, in Paris, accompanied by her footman, on her way to Notre Dame church, a poor man in religious garb suddenly joined them and entered into religious conversation. 'This man' says she, 'spoke to me in a wonderful manner of God and divine things.' He seemed to know all about her history, her virtues, and her faults. 'He gave me to understand,' says she, 'that God required not merely a heart of which it could only be said it is forgiven, but a heart which could properly, and in some real sense, be designated as holy, that it was not sufficient to escape hell, but that he demanded also the subjection of the evils of our nature, and the utmost purity and height of Christian attainment.' Concerning the effect of this conversation Madam Guyon says: "The Spirit of God bare witness to what he said. The words of this remarkable man... penetrated my soul. Deeply affected and overcome by what he had said, I had no sooner reached the church than I fainted away.'

"...Madam Guyon resolved that day before leaving the church, to give herself to the Lord anew... she resolved: From this day, this hour, if it be possible, I will be wholly the Lord's. The world shall have no portion in me.' Two years later she drew up and signed her historic Covenant of Consecration; but the real consecration seems to have been completed that day when she visited Notre Dame church. She yielded herself with reserve to the will of God, and almost immediately her consecration was tested by a series of overwhelming afflictions which served to purge out the dross that was in her nature. Her idols were destroyed one after another until all her hopes and joys and ambitions were centered in the Lord, and then He began to use her mightily in the building up of his kingdom" (pp. 97-98).

We cannot fully describe the afflictions and testings which God allowed her to go through, to cause her to die entirely to the self life. Briefly, she was stricken with smallpox which effaced her beauty; she lost her youngest son; in 1672 her beloved father died, and the same year her three year old daughter passed away. The death of her friend and counsellor, Genevieve Grainger, broke down another of her human props which caused her to lean more wholly on the Lord. In 1676 her husband who had become reconciled to her was taken away in death. But she saw the hand of God in all these things, that He was humbling her proud heart and will, purifying her soul of all dross. All this was climaxed by a seven year period of what she afterwards called her "state of privation, or desolation."

Father La Combe helped her by his letters. She appointed the 22nd of July, 1680, as a day in which Father La Combe should pray especially for her if her letter should reach him in time. Although he was a long way off, her letter reached him in time, so that both of them spent the whole day in prayer and fasting. Great deliverance came to her soul. Clouds of darkness lifted and floods of glory rolled through her soul. She says, "What I had possessed some years before, in the period of my spiritual enjoyment, was consolation, peace— the gift of God rather than the Giver; but now I was brought in such harmony with the will of God, that I might now be said to possess not merely consolation, but the *God* of consolation; not merely peace, but the *God* of peace. This true peace of mind was worth all that I had undergone, although it was only in its dawning."

Lawson quotes her further, in Torrents, where she says, "'...As a sanctified heart is always in harmony with the divine providences, I had no will but the divine will, of which such providences are the true and appropriate expression.' In another place she says: 'One characteristic of this higher experience was a sense of inward *purity*' ...She began to lead many others into the experience of sanctification through faith or into an experience of 'victory over the self life' or 'death to the self life,' as she was fond of calling it. Her soul was ablaze with the unction and power of the Holy Spirit, and everywhere she went she was besieged by multitudes of hungry, thirsty souls, who flocked to her for the spiritual meat which they failed to get from their regular pastors. Revivals of religion began in almost every place visited by her, and all over France earnest Christians began to seek the deeper experience taught by her" (*Op. Cit.*, pp. 102-103).

The Christian world knows more or less about this remarkable experience of Madam Guyon, although only a comparatively few spiritually discerning souls have realized that her second crisis was surely nothing less than what Wesley called "entire sanctification," or "Christian perfection." It is true that she approached this experience by degrees; but it is also true that there was a definite time when she exercised faith in God for immediate deliverance from inward foes; that she was victorious from that hour; and that she looked upon it as a crisis in her religious life. Wesley himself taught that there was usually a gradual approach to Christian perfection, and a gradual growth following the experience. This was exactly the case with Madam Guyon.

2. Fenelon.

A volume of interesting reading could be written on the experiences of Madam Guyon, Fenelon, Fox, and others whose experiences and writings influenced Wesley; but we believe that many of these are so well known to students of this subject, that only a brief mention of them will be practical here.

Fenelon, the devout and learned bishop of Cambray (1651-1715), was led by Madam Guyon into the higher experience and became a champion of the doctrine of "the interior life of self-crucifixion and pure love." He wrote a book entitled, *Maxims of the Saints Concerning the Interior Life*, in which he showed that the most eminent saints all down through the ages had experienced and taught this doctrine, if not formally at least informally. He quoted from such outstanding characters as St. Francis de Sales, St. Francis de Assisi, John of the Cross, Father Alvarez, St. Thomas Aquinas, St. Bernard, St. Theresa, Dionysius the Areopagite, Gregory Lopez, and many others. Needless to say his work, like that of Madam Guyon's, encountered fierce opposition and persecution from the Papacy, but it permeated France and the continent of Europe,— and has never ceased to yield its influence to the present day.

3. Fox and the Quakers.

George Fox and his co-laborers are often classed as among the later Mystics. His experience and teaching on the doctrine of Christian perfection is so well known that it is not necessary to take up space here to relate it. Probably no other denomination has continued to maintain the teaching of this doctrine over so long a period of its history, and among so large a percentage of its members and leaders, as has the Friends church.

Chapter XI
OTHER EMINENT CHRISTIAN WORTHIES WHO HELPED TO PREPARE THE WAY FOR WESLEYAN CHRISTIAN PERFECTION

1. Turretin and Witsius.

AMONG THE MANY PERSONS during the seventeenth century who embraced or at least approached the doctrine of Christian perfection in its evangelical sense, were two learned Presbyterian divines, Turretin and Witsius. In connection with the controversy between the Jansenists and the Jesuits, Dr. George Peck translates from the work of Turretin on *De Perfectione Sanctificationis*, vol. II, pp. 759, 760, as follows: "'The same question has been brought up anew in this age by the Neo-Pelagians, the Papists, the Socinians, and the Anabaptists, who have declared that the law can be perfectly fulfilled by the regenerate, that they might open the way for good works... It is to be observed, 1st. That the question is not concerning the perfection of sincerity... 2nd. It is not concerning perfection in extent. 3rd. It is not concerning comparative perfection, which is attributed to some believers who are more advanced than others, in which sense the believers of the New Testament are called perfect... 4th. It is not concerning evangelical perfection, which covers our imperfections with the garment of grace and the forbearance of the Father... since all those things which have been done are not imputed, while those which have not been done are pardoned, that is, covered by the righteousness of Christ, in whom we are said to be perfect. Col. 2:10. For all these kinds of perfection we acknowledge'" (*Christian Perfection*, pp. 118-119).

The same author proceeds to quote from Witsius, "'It cannot, indeed, be denied that sometimes the Scripture makes mention of some who are said to be perfect even in this life. But it is to be observed that the term perfection is not always used in the same sense. For, 1st. There is the perfection of sincerity... 2dly. There is a perfection of parts; and that both subjective... and objective... 3rdly. There is a comparative perfection ascribed to those who are advanced in knowledge, faith and sanctification, in comparison of those who are still infants and untaught... 4thly. There is also an evangelical perfection. 5thly, and lastly. There is also a perfection of degrees, by which a person performs all the commands of God... without the least defect... And this is that perfection which we deny the saints in this life, though we willingly allow them all the other kinds above mentioned'" (pp. 121-123). I quoted from *Economy of the Covenants*, vol. II, pp. 59, 60, Chap. 11, sec. 125. This sounds very much like Wesley.

2. Walter Marshall—

a Presbyterian who was fellow of New College, Oxford, and later fellow of Winchester, wrote a book entitled, *The Gospel Mystery of Sanctification* Opened in 1644, from which he is quoted in an editorial of the *Herald of Holiness*, May 25, 1932, as saying, "'Be sure to seek for holiness of heart and life only in its due order, where God hath placed it— after union with Christ, justification, and the gift of the Holy Ghost; and in that order seek it earnestly, by faith as a very necessary part of your salvation.'"

3. Cudworth, Lucas and Bunyan.—

In a sermon before the House of Commons the learned Cudworth, who died a short time before Wesley was born, said, "The end of the gospel is life and perfection; it is a divine nature; it is a God like frame, and disposition of spirit; it is to make us partakers of the image of God in righteousness and true holiness... I mean by holiness, nothing else but God stamped and printed upon my soul. True holiness is always breathing upward, and fluttering toward heaven, striving to embosom itself with God..."

Dr. Lucas, who died in 1715, wrote a treatise on "Religious Perfection," being the third part of his *Inquiry After Happiness* from which Wesley made an "extract" and included it in the twenty-fourth volume of his *Christian Library*. We quote a portion as follows:

"Religion is nothing else but the purifying and refining nature by grace, the raising and exalting our faculties and capacities by wisdom and virtue. Religious perfection, therefore, is nothing else but the moral accomplishment of human nature; such a maturity of virtue as man in this life is capable of; conversion begins, perfection consummates the habit of righteousness: in the one, religion is as it were in its infancy; in the other, in its strength and manhood; so that perfection, in short, is nothing else but a ripe and settled habit of true holiness... The doctrine of infused habits has been much ridiculed and exposed, as absurd, by some men... But why God cannot produce in us those strong dispositions to virtue in a moment, which are ordinarily produced by time; or why we may not ascribe as much efficiency to infused habits, as philosophers are wont to do to repeated acts, I cannot see. Nor can I see why such dispositions, when infused, may not be called habits, if they have all the properties and effects of a habit."

Bunyan, a Baptist, in his immortal *Pilgrim's Progress* represents the work of sanctification at the "Interpreter's House," according to Jas. Alex. McDonald. He quotes regarding "The Bath of Sanctification," "'The Interpreter would have them tarry a while... Take them and have them into the garden to the bath, and there wash them, and make them clean from the soil which they have gathered by traveling.'" Then is described by Bunyan the putting on them of a "seal," of white linen garments, how they shone so brightly that, "'they seemed to be a terror one to the other; for that they could not see that glory each one had in himself, which they could see in each other. Now, therefore, they began to esteem each other better than themselves'" (pp. 93-94).

To the same point is Rev. J.P. Taylor's citation of Bunyan's experience, in his article in the *Free Methodist* of December 4, 1931: "The celebrated Pilgrim after various fortunes and misfortunes arrived in the 'country of Beulah,' and he with his companions 'heard continually the singing birds, and saw every day the flowers appear in the earth... In this country the sun shineth day and night.' Here they were 'also out of reach of Giant Despair; neither could they from this place so much as see Doubting Castle. Here they were within sight of the City they were going to, also here met them some of the inhabitants thereof; for in this land the Shining Ones commonly walked, because it was upon the borders of heaven. In this land also the contract between the bride and Bridegroom was renewed... Here they had no want of corn and wine; for in this place they met with abundance of what they had sought for in all their pilgrimage... Here all the inhabitants of the country called them 'the holy people;' 'the redeemed of the Lord'... As they walked in this land they had more rejoicing than in parts more remote from the Kingdom to which they were bound; and drawing near to the City, 'they had yet a more perfect view thereof' ... It is regrettable that the dreamer did not discover the land of Beulah at an earlier stage of the journey and save his pilgrim from some aberrations and near-disasters to which the unsanctified are always exposed."

4. Taylor, Kempis, Law.—

We now come to the men who probably influenced Wesley the most in his arriving at the doctrine of Christian perfection. This we think is so well known by those who are at all posted on the subject that we need not go into detail, but will give the record as related by Wesley himself in the first part of his *A Plain Account of Christian Perfection*, as follows: "1. What I purpose in the following paper is, to give a plain and distinct account of the steps by which I was led, during a course of many years, to embrace the doctrine of Christian perfection.

"2. In the year 1725, being in the twenty-third year of my age, I met with Bishop Taylor's *Rules and Exercises of Holy Living and Dying*... Instantly I resolved to dedicate all my life to God, all my thoughts, and words, and actions...

"3. In the year 1726, I met with Kempis' *Christian's Pattern*. The nature and extent of inward religion, the religion of the heart, now appeared to me in a stronger light than ever it had done before. I saw that giving even all my life to God... would profit me nothing, unless I gave my heart, yea, all my heart to him. I saw that 'simplicity of intention, and purity of affection,' one design in all that we speak or do, and one desire ruling all our tempers, are indeed 'the wings of the soul,' without which she can never ascend to the mount of God.

"4. A year or two after, Mr. Law's *Christian Pattern and Serious Call* were put into my hands. These convinced me more than ever, of the absolute impossibility of being half a Christian; and I determined, through his grace, (the absolute necessity of which I was deeply sensible,) to be all devoted to God, to give him all my soul, my body, and my substance.

"5. In the year 1729, I began not only to read, but to study the Bible, as the one, the only standard of truth, and the only model of true religion. Hence I saw, in a clearer and clearer light, the indispensable necessity of having 'the mind which is in Christ,' and of 'walking as Christ also walked;' even of having, not some part only, but all the mind which was in him; and of walking as he walked, not only in many or most respects, but in all things...

"6. On January 1, 1733, I preached before the university, in St. Mary's church, on 'the circumcision of the heart,' an account of which I gave in these words: 'It is that habitual disposition of soul which, in the sacred writings, is termed holiness; and which directly implies the being cleansed from sin, "from all filthiness both of flesh and spirit," and, by consequence, the being endued with those virtues which were in Christ; the being so "renewed in the image of our mind" as to be "perfect as our Father which is in heaven is perfect"' (Works, vol. 1, p. 148, Am. edit).

"In the same sermon I observed, "'Love is the fulfilling of the law, the end of the commandment." It is not only "the first and great" command, but all the commandments in one. "Whatsoever things are just, whatsoever things are pure, if there be any virtue, if there be any praise," they are all comprised in this one word, love. In this is perfection, and glory, and happiness: the royal law of heaven and earth is this, "Thou shalt love the Lord thy God with all thy heart, and with all thy soul, and with all thy mind, and with all thy strength..."

"It may be observed, this sermon was composed the first of all my writings which have been published. This was the view of religion I then had, which even then I scrupled not to call perfection. This is the view I have of it now, without any material addition or diminution."

"7. In the same sentiment did my brother and I remain (with all those young gentlemen in derision termed *Methodists*) till we embarked for America, in the latter end of 1735...

"8. In August following [in 1738], I had a long conversation with Arvid Gradin, in Germany. After he had given me an account of his experience, I desired him to give me, in writing, a definition of 'the full assurance of faith,' which he did in the following words:— [we omit the Latin version and give merely the English translation,] 'Repose in the blood of Christ, a firm confidence in God, and persuasion of his favour; the highest tranquility, serenity, and peace of mind, with a deliverance from every fleshly desire, and a cessation of all, even inward sins.'

"This was the first account I ever heard from any living man, of what I had before learned from the oracles of God, and had been praying for, (with the little company of my friends,) and expecting, for several years.

"9. In 1739, my brother and I published a volume of "Hymns and Sacred Poems.' In many of these we declared our sentiments strongly and explicitly...

"10. The first tract I ever wrote expressly on this subject was published in the latter end of this year. That none might be prejudiced before they read it, I gave it the indifferent title of 'The Character of a Methodist.' In this I described a perfect Christian, placing in the front, 'Not as though I had already 'attained.' Part of it I subjoin without any alteration:

"'A Methodist is one who loves the Lord his God with all his heart, with all his soul, with all his mind, and with all his strength... Perfect love having cast out fear, he rejoices evermore... He loves his enemies, yea, and the enemies of God... For he is "pure in heart." Love has purified his heart from envy, malice, wrath, and every unkind temper. It has cleansed him from pride, whereof "only comest contention;" and he hath now "put on bowels of mercies, kindness, humbleness of mind, meekness, long suffering." And indeed all possible ground for contention, on his part, is cut off...

"'All the commandments of God he accordingly keeps, and that with all his might; for his obedience is in proportion to his love, the source from whence it flows. And, therefore, loving God with all his heart, he serves him with all his strength... All the talents he has, he constantly employs according to his Master's will; every power and faculty of his soul, every member of his body.'

"These are the very words wherein I largely declared, for the first time, my sentiments of Christian perfection. And is it not easy to see, (1) That this is the very point at which I aimed all along from the year 1725; and more determinately from the year 1730... (2) That this is the very same doctrine which I believe and teach at this day; not adding one point, either to that inner or outward holiness which I maintained eight-and-thirty years ago.

"11. I do not know that any writer has made any objection against that tract to this day; and for some time I did not find much opposition upon the head, at least, not from serious persons. But, after a time, a cry arose...

"12. I think it was in the latter end of the year 1740, that I had a conversation with Dr. Gibson, then bishop of London, at Whitehall. He asked me what I meant by perfection. I told him without any disguise or reserve. When I ceased speaking, he said, 'Mr. Wesley, if this be all you mean, publish it to all the world. If any one then can confute what you say, he may have free leave.' I answered, 'My Lord, I will,' and accordingly wrote and published the sermon on Christian perfection."

Chapter XII
THE MORAVIAN PENTECOST

WE WILL CLOSE THIS WORK by recounting the wonderful outpouring of the Holy Spirit on the Moravians at Herrnhut, August 13, 1727, which was in some respects a repetition of Pentecost. This remarkable experience transformed and empowered a small group of comparatively weak and diverse Christians, until they went forth as fiery evangels witnessing for Christ with such zeal and boldness that their influence went out unto the uttermost parts of the earth. It resulted in a rebirth and the actual making of the Moravian church which immediately began to send forth foreign missionaries fifty years before the time of modem missions under Carey; it was influential in the conversion of John and Charles Wesley; and produced a great wealth of Christian hymns.

While Count Zinzendorf, the leader of the Moravians, and his followers, never advanced the doctrine of Christian perfection as afterwards formulated by Wesley, their experience at Herrnhut was certainly similar if not identical with the experience of entire sanctification as taught by the Methodists. Rev. John Greenfield of Warsaw, Indiana, wrote an interesting account of this incident in a book entitled, *Power from on High* on the occasion of the two hundredth anniversary of the Moravian revival, from which we will quote:

"...We are now celebrating the Bicentennial of what our Moravian Text Book calls the 'Signal out-pouring of the Holy Spirit experienced by the congregation of Herrnhut'... A Moravian historian writes... as follows: 'God says: It shall come to pass— I will pour.' This was His promise through the prophet Joel. The first fulfillment of this promise was on the day of Pentecost. There is nothing in the New Testament to indicate that this was to 'be the one and only fulfillment of this promise... Church history also abounds in records of special outpourings of the Holy Ghost, and verily the thirteenth of August, 1727, was a day of the outpouring of the Holy Spirit. We saw the hand of God and his wonders, and we were all under the cloud of our fathers baptized with their spirit. The Holy Ghost came upon us and in those days great signs and wonders took place in our midst. From that time scarcely a day passed but what we beheld His almighty workings amongst us. A great hunger after the Word of God took possession of us so that we had to have three services every day... Everyone desired above everything else that the Holy Spirit might have full control. Self-love and self-will as well as all disobedience disappeared and an overwhelming flood of grace swept us all out into the great ocean of Divine Love.'

"Exactly what happened that Wednesday forenoon, August 13th, 1727, in the specially called Communion service at Berthelsdorf, none of the participants could fully describe. They left the house of God that noon 'hardly knowing whether they belonged to earth or had already gone to Heaven'" (p. 9-11).

XII: The Moravian Pentecost

Greenfield quotes from a summary by Bishop Edward Rondthaler: "'Zinzendorf, who gives us the deepest and most vivid account of this wonderful occurrence, says it was "a sense of the nearness of Christ" bestowed in a single moment upon all the members that were present: and it was so unanimous that two members, at work twenty miles away, unaware that the meeting was being held, became at the same time, deeply conscious of the same blessing.'

"'These members were all laity, though at a later time, ministers and missionaries, deacons, presbyters and bishops arose out of the wonderfully blessed assemblage...

"'It was a young congregation which received the 13th of August blessing. Zinzendorf, the human leader, was just twenty-seven years old, and if a census had been taken, it would have been found that his own age was approximately the average of the whole company...' (pp. 11-12).

"The spiritual experiences of the Moravian brethren two centuries ago bear a striking resemblance to the Pentecostal power and results in the days of the Apostles. The company of believers 'both at Jerusalem and Herrnhut numbered less than three hundred souls. Both congregations were humanly speaking totally devoid of worldly influence, wisdom, power and wealth... At once these believers, naturally timid and fearful, were transformed into flaming evangelists. Supernatural knowledge and power seemed to possess them...

"...During the first three decades after their spiritual Pentecost they carried the gospel of salvation... not only to nearly every country in Europe but also to many pagan races in America, North and South, Asia and Africa" (pp. 12-14).

The unpromising condition of the company at Herrnhut with their differences of opinion and heated controversy on doctrinal questions before this outpouring of the Spirit, and how Count Zinzendorf prepared them for this enduing, is related:

"The first part of the year 1727 did not seem very promising. Differences of opinion and heated controversy on doctrinal questions threatened to disrupt the congregation. The majority were members of the Ancient Moravian Church of the Brethren. But other believers had also been attracted to Herrnhut. Lutherans, Reformed, Baptists, etc., had joined the community. Questions of predestination, holiness, the meaning and mode of baptism, etc., etc., seemed likely to divide the believers into a number of small and belligerent sects. Then the more earnest and spiritual souls among them began to cry mightily unto the Lord for deliverance. His first answer was a general outpouring upon them of 'the spirit of grace and supplication.' (Zech. 12:10).

"...He also sent them a human leader and deliverer in the person of the young German nobleman, Count Zinzendorf, who so kindly had offered this persecuted church a place of refuge on his own estates. This godly youth and pre-eminent genius had been divinely prepared for his great work of spiritual leadership... Count Zinzendorf had early learned the secret of prevailing prayer. So active had he been in establishing circles for prayer, that on leaving the college at Halle, sixteen years of age, he handed the famous Professor Francke a list of seven praying societies... It was a condition and not a theory which confronted the young nobleman in 1727 at Herrnhut. How to unite in faith and love and service the pious but disputatious followers of Huss, Luther, Calvin, Zwingle, Schwenkfeld, etc., etc., seemed indeed a hopeless problem apart from divine intervention. In answer to earnest and persevering prayer superhuman wisdom guided the young Count in the use of certain means which proved of incalculable value. Bishop J.T. Hamilton has called attention to this in a recent article in the *Moravian*. After describing the Brotherly Covenant drawn up by Zinzendorf calling upon them 'to seek out and emphasize the points in which they agreed' rather than to stress their differences, and the Count's personal interview with every individual adult resident in Herrnhut, Bishop Hamilton says:

"'But far more important than this was their entering into solemn covenant with Zinzendorf, that twelfth of May, to actually dedicate their lives, as he dedicated his, to the service of the Lord Jesus Christ, each one in his particular calling and position. This covenant was in essentials what constitutes our Brotherly Agreement of today...

"'There followed the choice of the twelve elders to complete the organization of the spiritual life of Herrnhut, and the appointment of persons to the various offices foreseen in the statutes. So order, itself a product of greater mutual confidence as well as of mutually recognized devotion, made possible provision for the Bible study and the frequent gathering of bands for prayer, that next marked the ensuing summer months and led the way to and prepared the way for the baptism of the Spirit that culminated on that Blessed thirteenth of August, an enduement with power, that enabled those men and women of Herrnhut to serve their generation so effectively...' pp. 19-22.

"Truly the great Moravian revival of 1727, which reached its climax August 13, was preceded and followed by most extraordinary praying. The spirit of grace and supplications manifested itself in the early part of the year. Count Zinzendorf began to give spiritual instructions to a class of nine girls between the ages of ten and thirteen years. 'The Count' so the historian of that period tells us, 'frequently complained to his consort that though the children behaved with great outward propriety, he could not perceive any traces of spiritual life among them; and however much might be said to them of the Lord Jesus Christ, yet it did not seem to reach their hearts. In this distress of his mind he took his refuge to the Lord in prayer, most fervently entreating Him to grant to these children His grace and blessing.'

"What a spectacle! A gifted, wealthy, young German nobleman on his knees, agonizing in prayer for the conversion of some little school girls! Later on we read as follows:

"'July 16. The Count poured forth his soul in a heart-affecting prayer, accompanied with a flood of tears; this prayer produced an extraordinary effect, and was the beginning of the subsequent operation of the life-giving and energetic Spirit of God.'" Not only Count Zinzendorf, but many other brethren also began to pray as never before. In the 'Memorial Days of the Renewed Moravian Church,' we read as follows:

"'July 22.— A number of Brethren covenanted together of their own accord, engaging to meet often on the Hutberg, to pour out their hearts in prayer and hymns.

"'On the fifth of August the Warden, viz., the Count, spent the whole night in watching, in company of about twelve or fourteen brethren. At mid-night there was held on the Hutberg a large meeting for the purpose of prayer, at which great emotion prevailed.'

"'On Sunday, August 10, about noon, while Pastor Rothe was holding the meeting at Herrnhut, he felt himself overwhelmed by a wonderful and irresistible power of the Lord, and sunk down into the dust before God, and with him sunk down the whole assembled congregation, in an ecstasy of feeling. In this frame of mind they continued until midnight en-

XII: The Moravian Pentecost

gaged in prayer and singing, weeping and supplication.

"'After that distinguished day of blessing, the 13th day of August, 1727... the thought struck some brethren and sisters that it might be well to set apart certain hours for the purpose of prayer, at which seasons all might be reminded of its excellency, and be induced by the promise annexed to fervent prayer to pour out their hearts before the Lord.

"'It was moreover considered as an important point that, as in the days of the Old Covenant, the sacred fire was never permitted to go out on the altar (Lev. 6:13 and 14), so in a congregation which is a temple of the living God, wherein He has His altar and His fire, the intercession of His saints should incessantly rise up unto Him like holy incense.

"'On August 26 twenty-four brethren and the same number of sisters met, and covenanted together to continue from one midnight to the next in prayer, dividing for that purpose the twenty-four hours of night and day by lot among themselves.

"'August 27 this new regulation was put into practice. More were soon added to this number of intercessors, which was thus increased to seventy-seven, and even the awakened children began a plan similar to this among themselves. Everyone carefully observed the hour which had been appointed for them. The Intercessors had a weekly meeting, at which notice was given them of those things which they were to consider special subjects for prayer and remembrance before the Lord.

"'The children of both sexes felt a most powerful impulse to prayer, and it was impossible to listen to their infant supplications without being deeply moved and affected. A blessed meeting of the children took place in the evening of the 26th of August, and on the 29th, from the hours of ten o'clock at night until one the following morning a truly affecting scene was witnessed for the girls of Herrnhut and Berthelsdorf spent these hours in praying, singing and weeping on the Hutberg. The boys were at the same time engaged in earnest prayer in another place. The spirit of prayer and supplication at that time poured out upon the children was so powerful and efficacious that it is impossible to give an adequate description of it in words. These were truly days of heavenly enjoyment to the congregation at Herrnhut; all forgot themselves, and things terrestrial and transitory and longed to be above with Christ, in bliss everlasting.'"

Another eyewitness says:

"'I cannot ascribe the cause of the great awakening of the children at Herrnhut to anything but the wonderful outpouring of the Spirit of God upon the communicant congregation assembled on that occasion. The breezes of the Spirit pervaded at that time equally both young and old.'"

"Again we quote from Bishop Evelyn Hasse: 'Was there ever in the whole of church history such an astonishing prayer-meeting as that which beginning in 1727, went on one hundred years. It is something absolutely unique. It was known as the "Hourly Intercession," and it meant that by relays of Brethren and Sisters prayer without ceasing was made to God for all the work and wants of His church. Prayer of that kind always leads to action. In this case it kindled a burning desire to make Christ's Salvation known to the heathen. It led to the beginning of Foreign Missions. From that one small village community more than "one hundred missionaries went out in twenty-five years. You will look in vain elsewhere for anything to match it in anything like the same extent'" (pp. 23-26).

While the Moravians did not from this remarkable experience formulate a particular doctrine of Christian perfection or entire sanctification as a second crisis in the life of believers, as Wesley did, it certainly amounted to the same thing essentially. They did teach what they called, "The full assurance of faith," which Arvid Gradin, one of their leaders defined to Wesley, as we have already seen (ante 69 and 70) in the following words: 'Repose in the blood of Christ; a firm confidence in God, and persuasion in his favour; the highest tranquility, serenity, and peace of mind, with a deliverance from every fleshly desire, and a cessation of all, even inward sins.' That was not the experience of the Moravians before August 13, 1727, but it was after that outpouring of the Spirit. Evidently Wesley recognized that fact because after referring to Gradin's definition of "the full assurance of faith," Wesley says: "That was the first account I ever heard from any living man, of what I had before learned myself from the oracles of God, and had been praying for, (with the little company of my friends,) and expecting for several years." Wesley was here speaking with reference to "the steps by which I was led, during a course of many years, to embrace the doctrine of Christian perfection." —Wesley's *Christian Perfection*.

Conclusion

WE HAVE TRACED at least some of the outstanding experiences and testimonies of eminent saints of all periods of the church down to the time of Wesley, to determine what historical background the Wesleyans had for the formulation of the doctrine of Christian perfection. We believe it is clear that this was not a new idea, but rather was more or less prevalent, though stated in various ways, during all ages of Christendom. Wesley and his followers elaborated the doctrine more thoroughly than what had been done up to this time; defined it more sharply; and stressed it more fully as an ideal and experience not only desirable but attainable in this life.

BIBLIOGRAPHY

Baldwin, Rev. H.A., "Entire Sanctification a Biblical, Historical and Experimental Fact" —a series of three articles published in *The Free Methodist* in the January 15th, 22nd and 29th numbers, 1932.

Brooks, Dr. John R., *Scriptural Sanctification*.

Clark, Dr. Adam, quoted by Dr. George Peck in *Christian Perfection*.

Fletcher, John, *Christian Perfection*.

Greenfield, Rev. John, "Power from on High."

Herald of Holiness, May 25, 1932.

Lawson, Dr. J. Gilchrist, *Deeper Experiences of Famous Christians*.

McDonald, James Alex, *Wesley's Revision of the Shorter Catechism*.

Peck, Dr. George, *Christian Perfection*.

Scougal, Henry, "Life of God in the Soul of Man."

Taylor, Rev. J.P., "Holiness the Doctrine of Antiquity" —two articles in *The Free Methodist*, December, 1932.

Theologica Germanica.

Wesley, John, *A Plain Account of Christian Perfection*.

Members of Schmul's Wesleyan Book Club buy these outstanding books at 40% off the retail price.

Join Schmul's Wesleyan Book Club by calling toll-free:
800-S$_7$P$_7$B$_2$O$_6$O$_6$K$_5$S$_7$
Put a discount Christian bookstore in your own mailbox.

Visit us on the Internet at
www.wesleyanbooks.com

You may also order direct from the publisher by writing:
Schmul Publishing Company
PO Box 776
Nicholasville, KY 40340

www.ingramcontent.com/pod-product-compliance
Lightning Source LLC
Chambersburg PA
CBHW071316040426
42444CB00009B/2030